Amazing Swear

Hilarious Sweary Coloring Book

By

S.B. Nozaz

Copyright © 2016 by S.B. Nozaz

All rights reserved worldwide. No part of this publication may be reproduced or distributed in any form or by any means, mechanical, electronic or stored in a retrieval or database system, without written permission from the copyright holder.

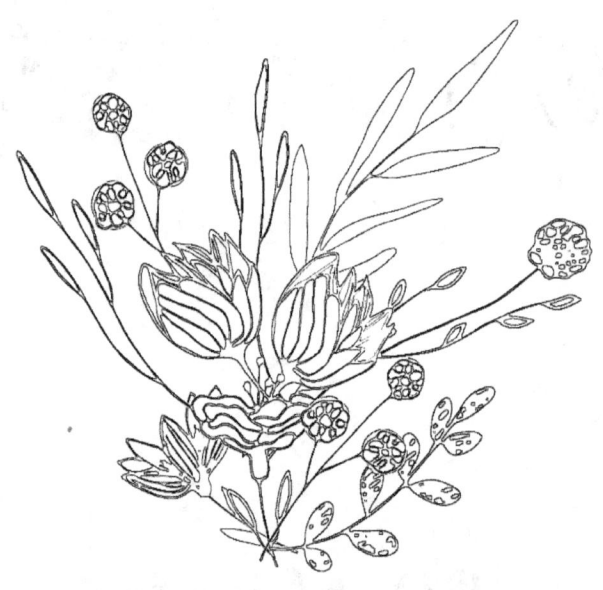

Happy Coloring!

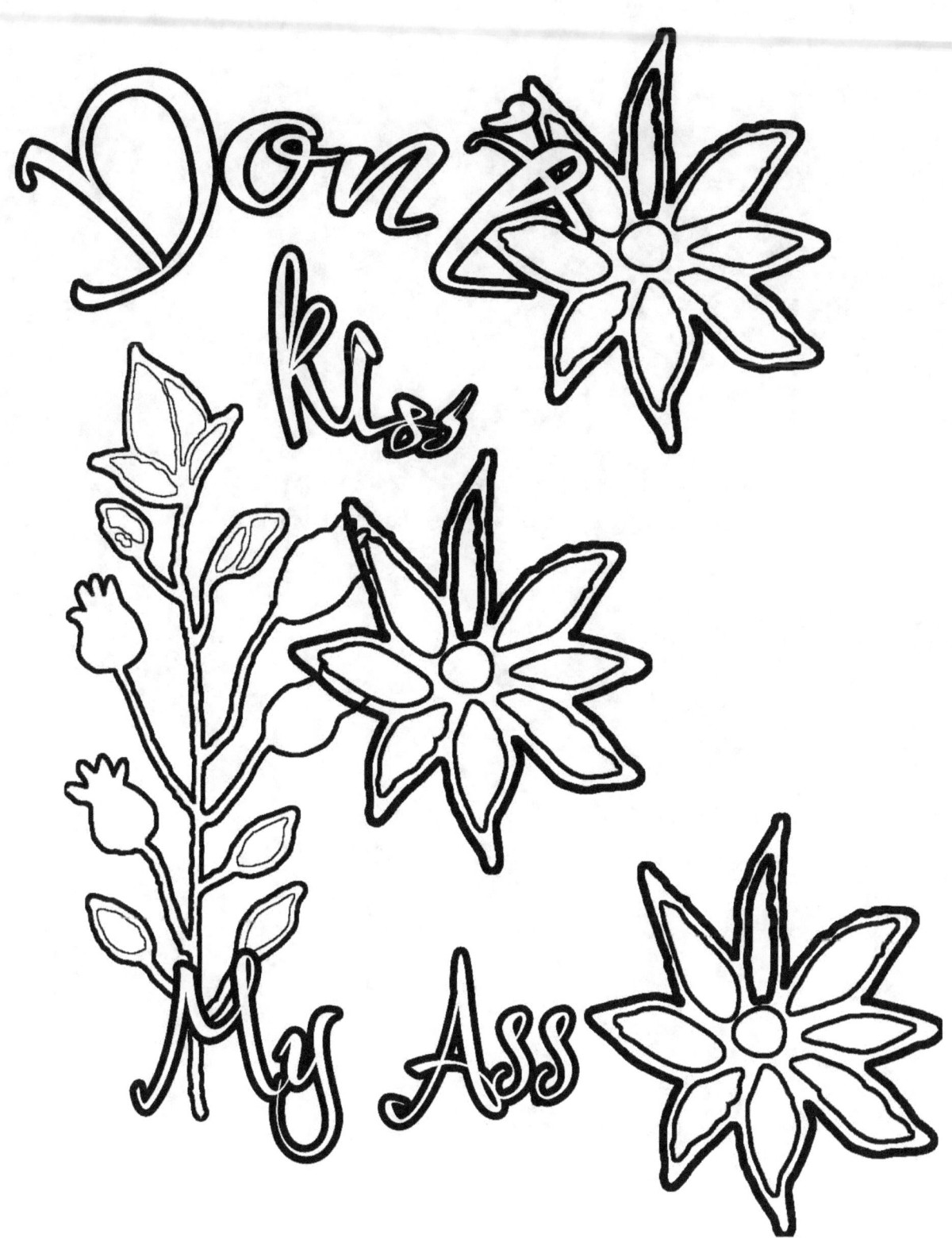

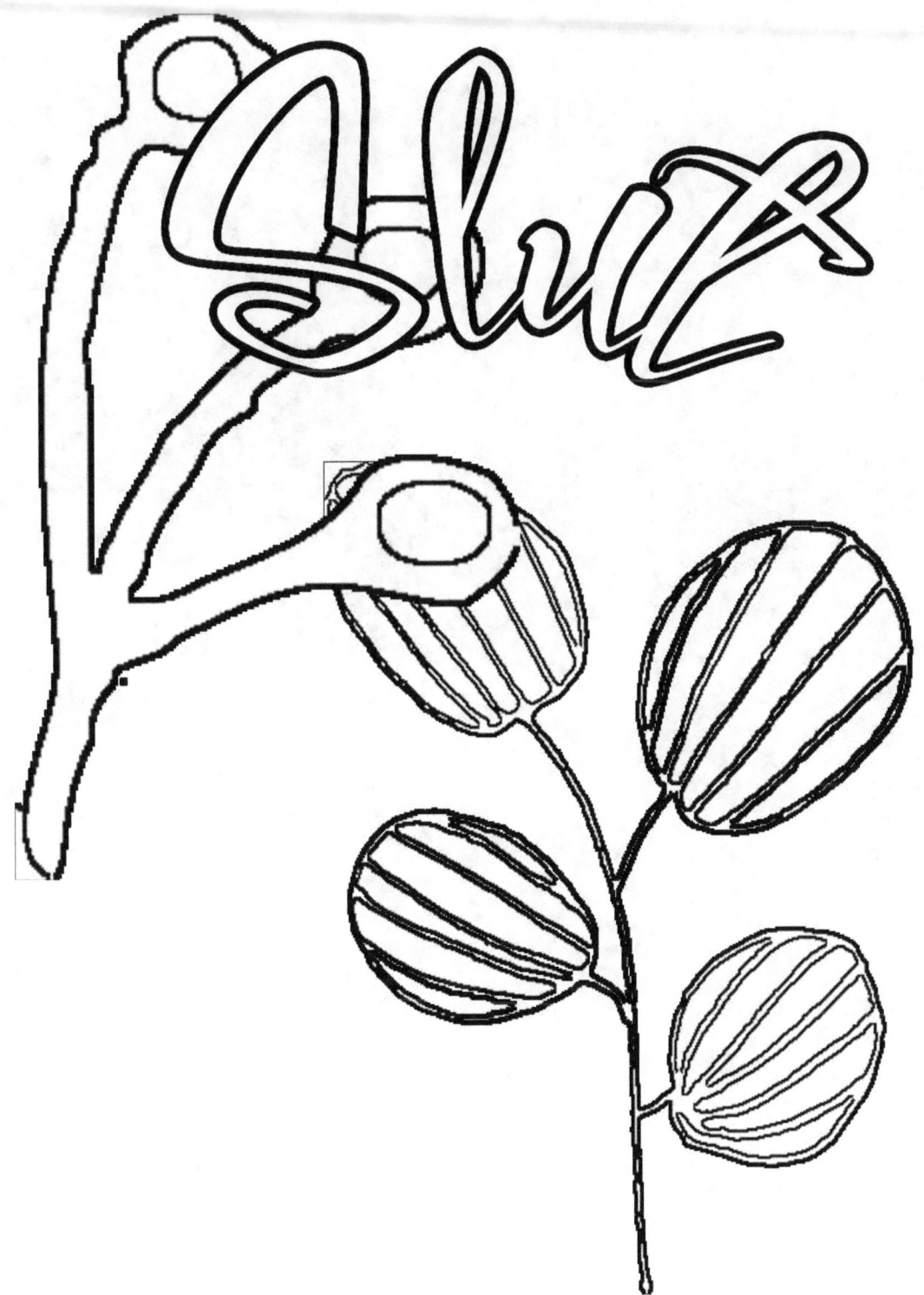

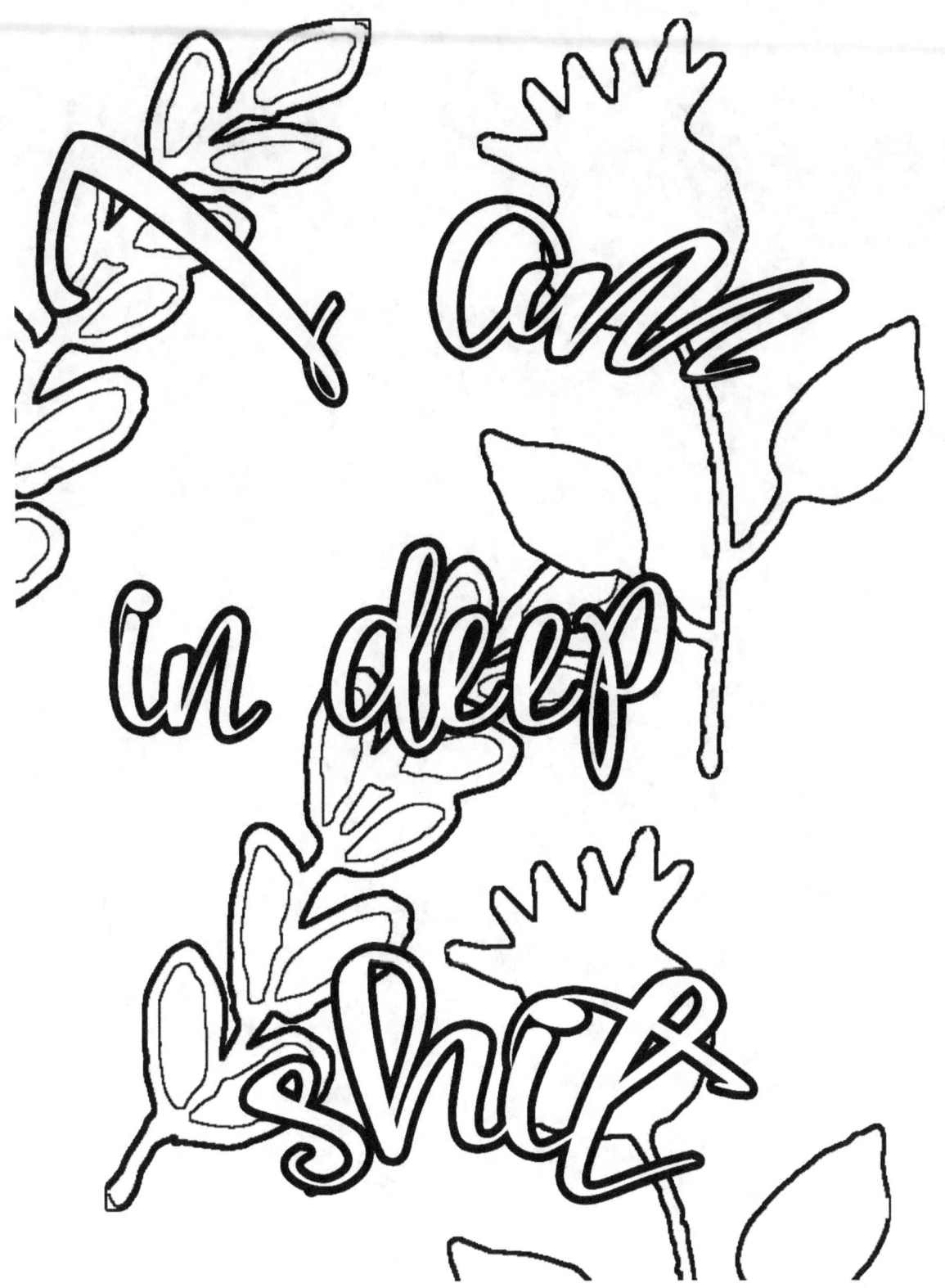

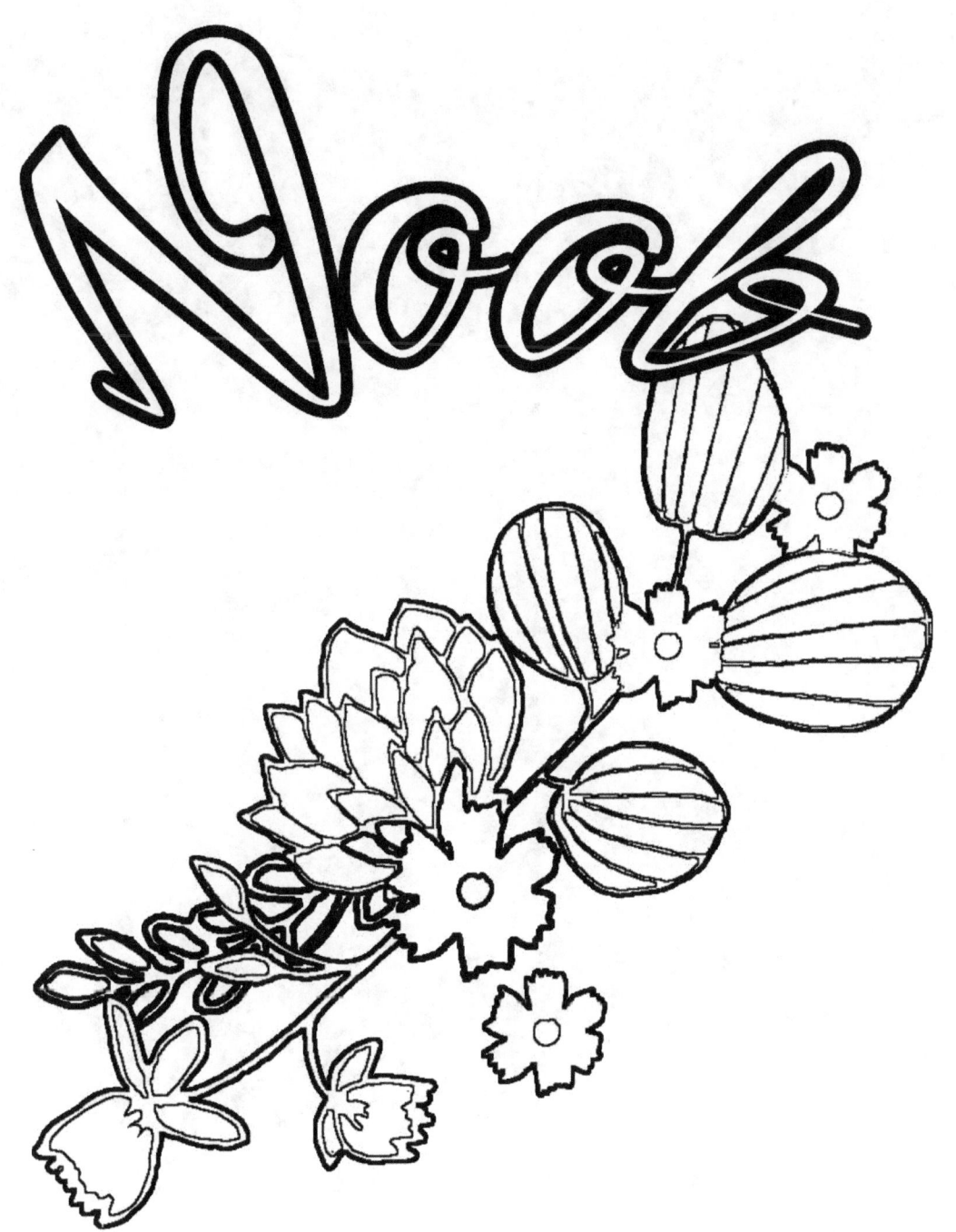

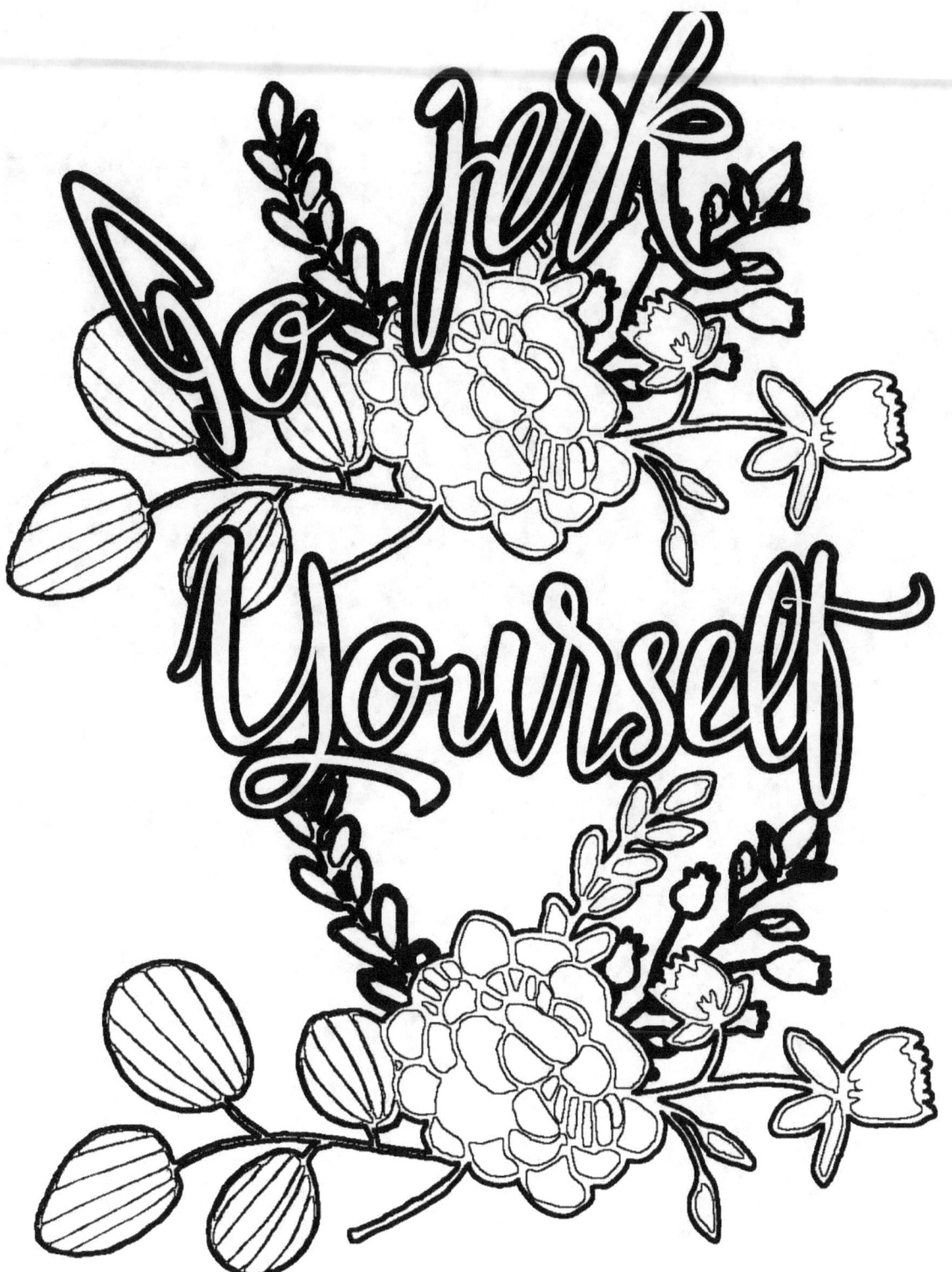

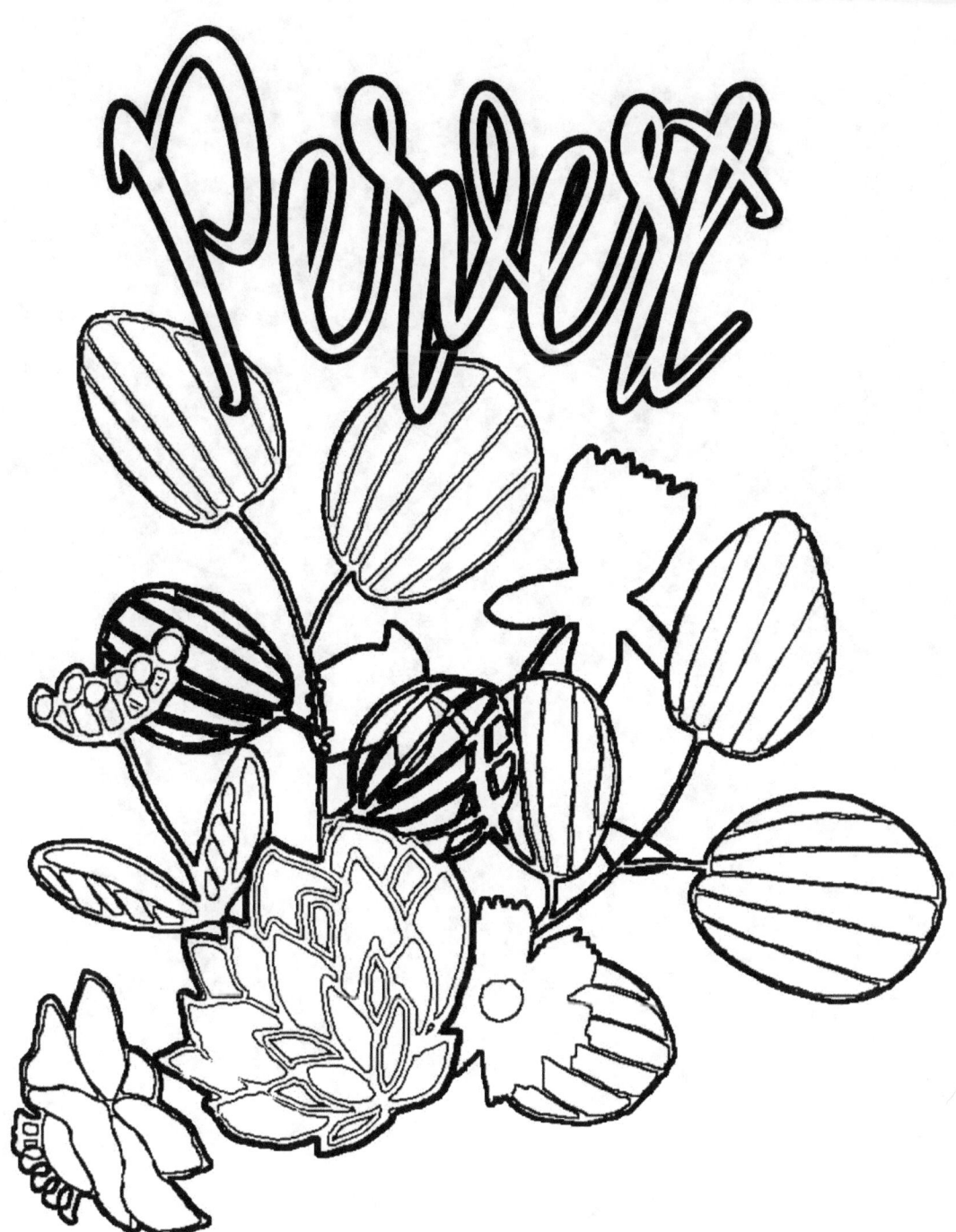

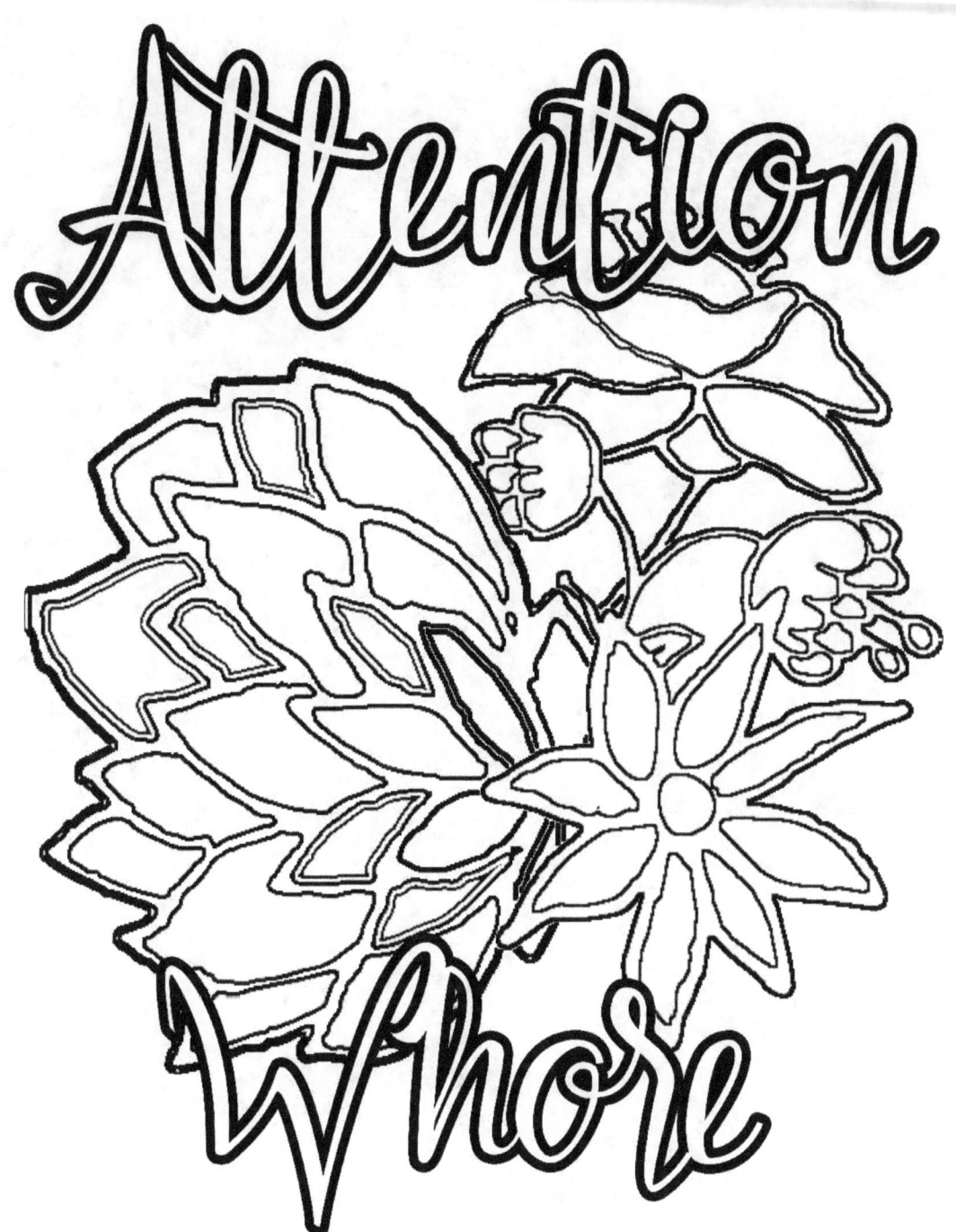

Fuck A Duck

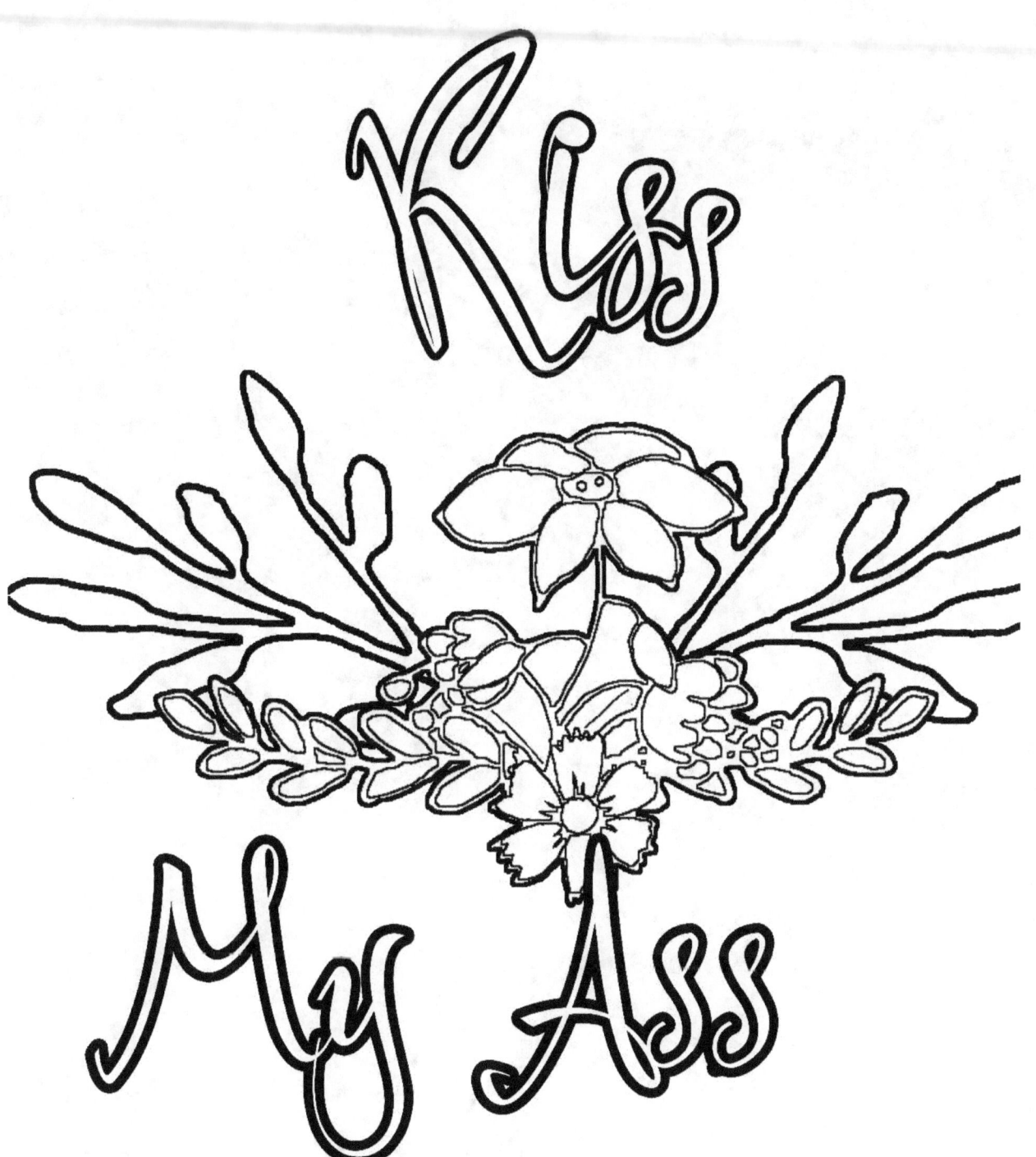

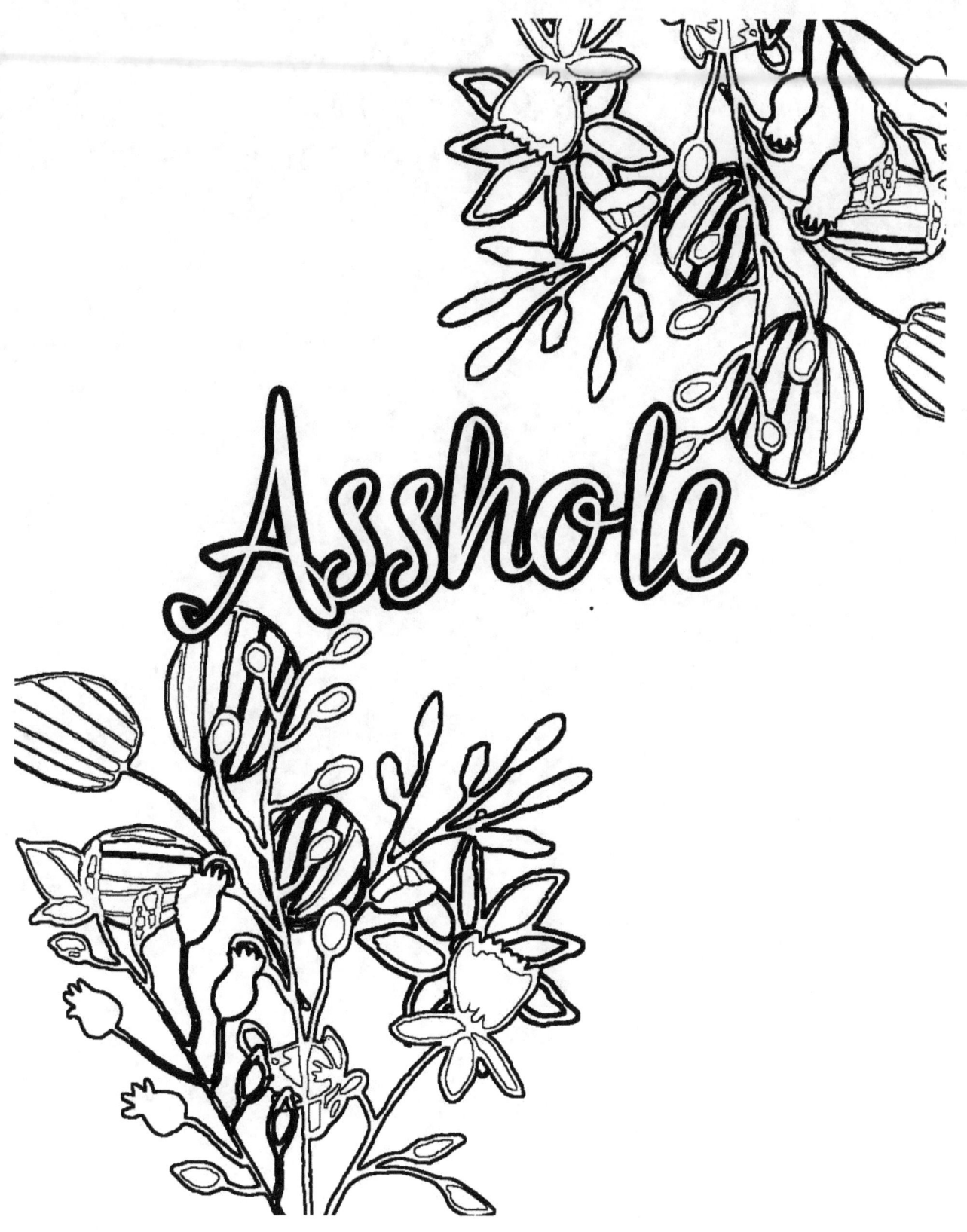

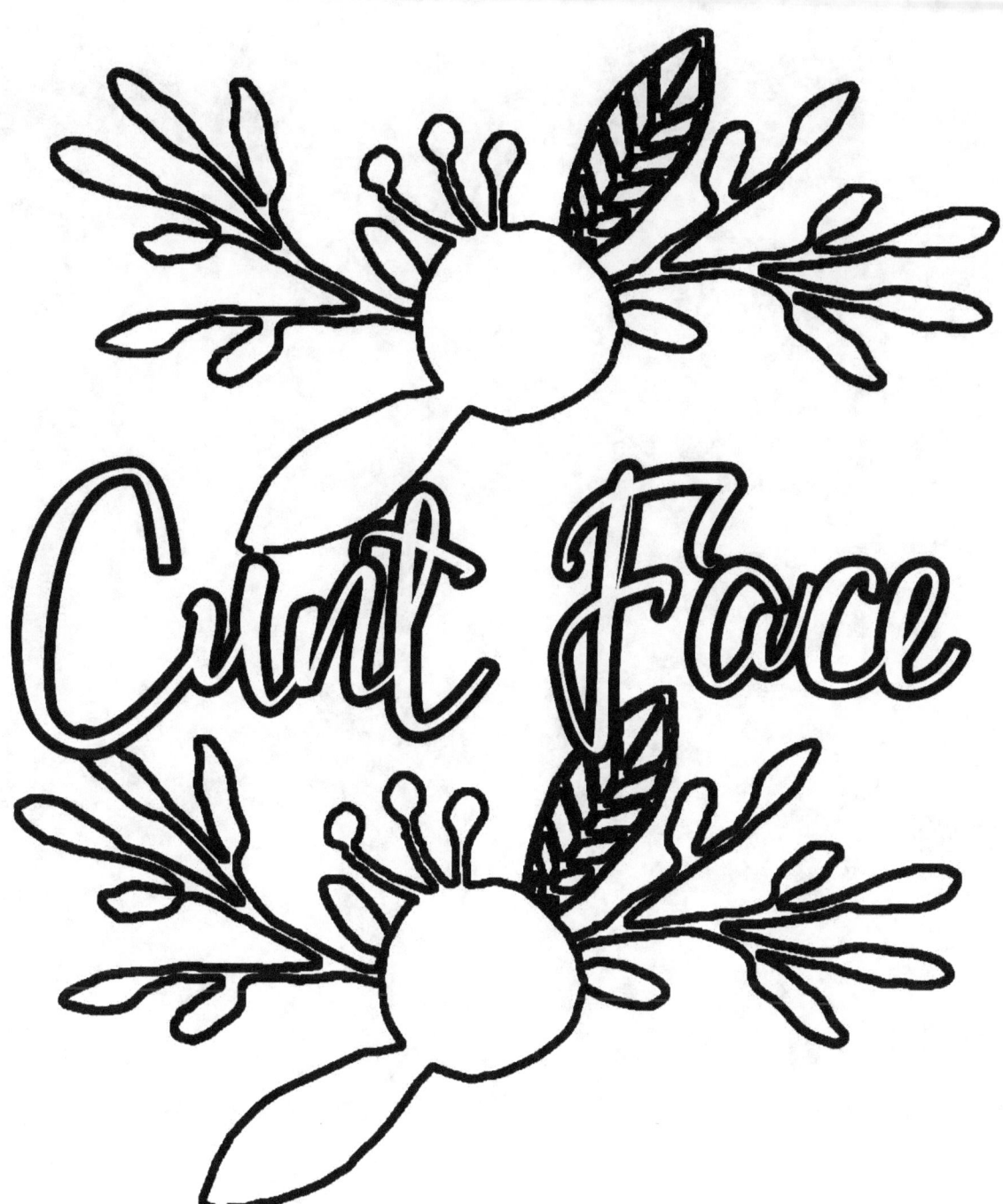

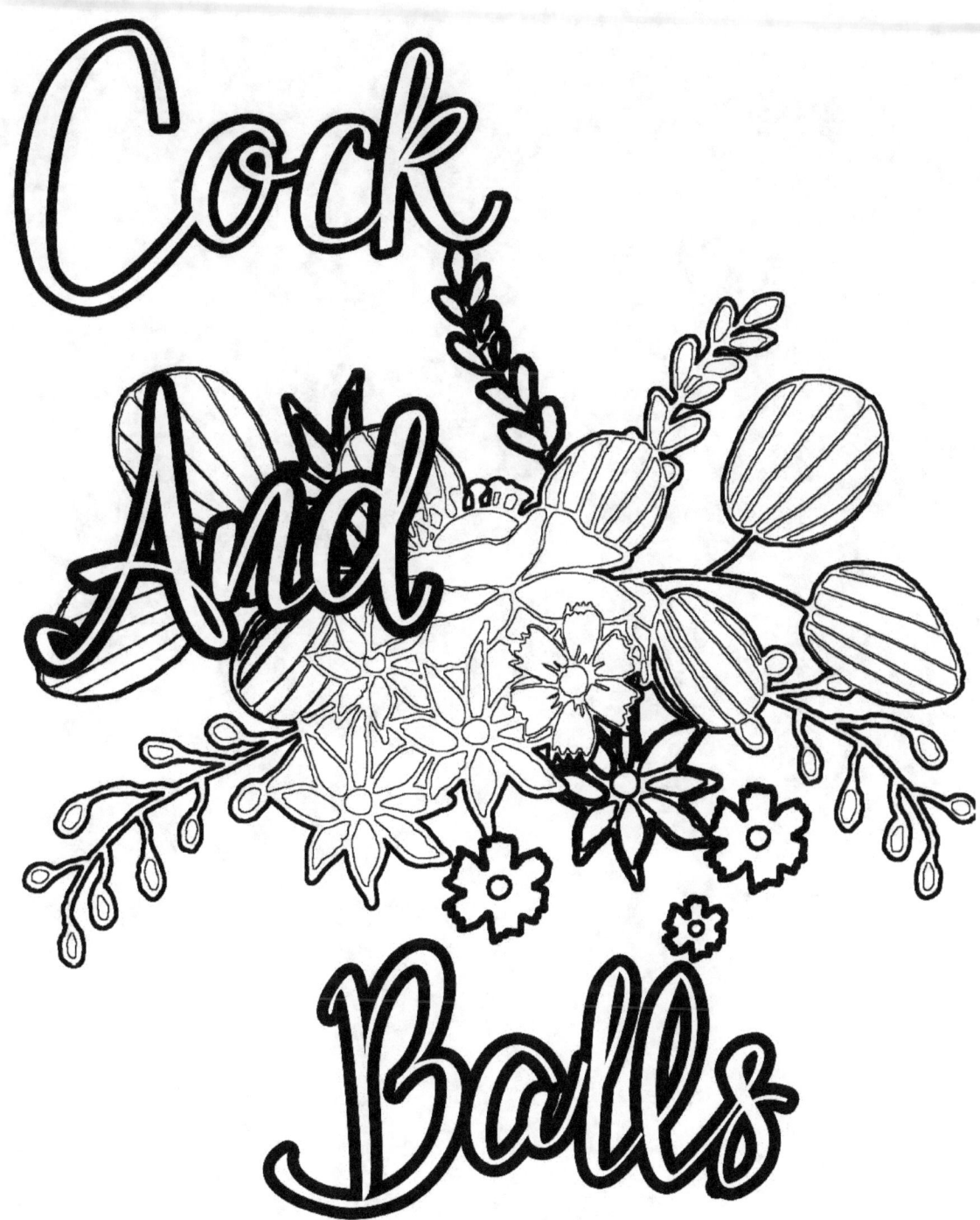

Bastard

Whore

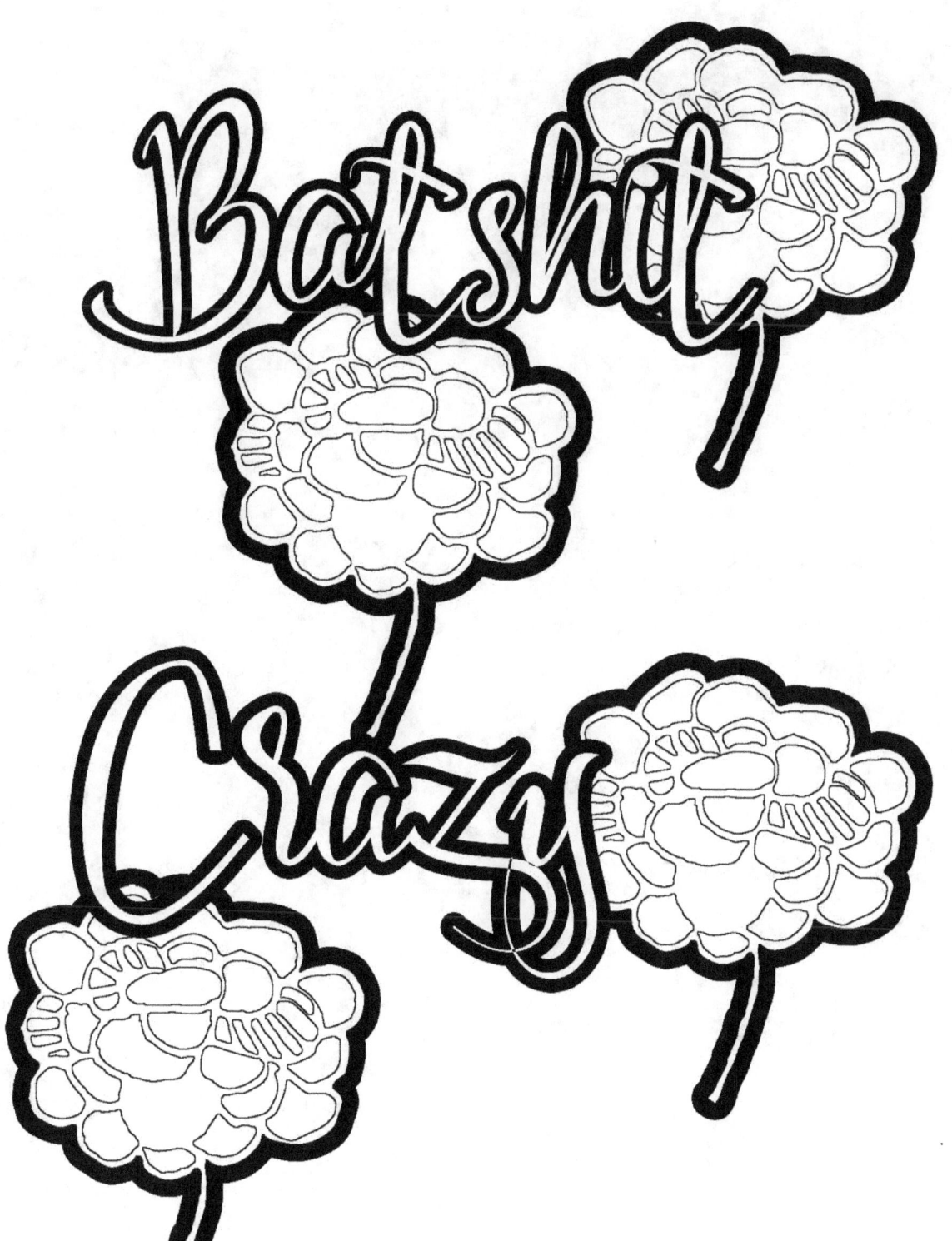

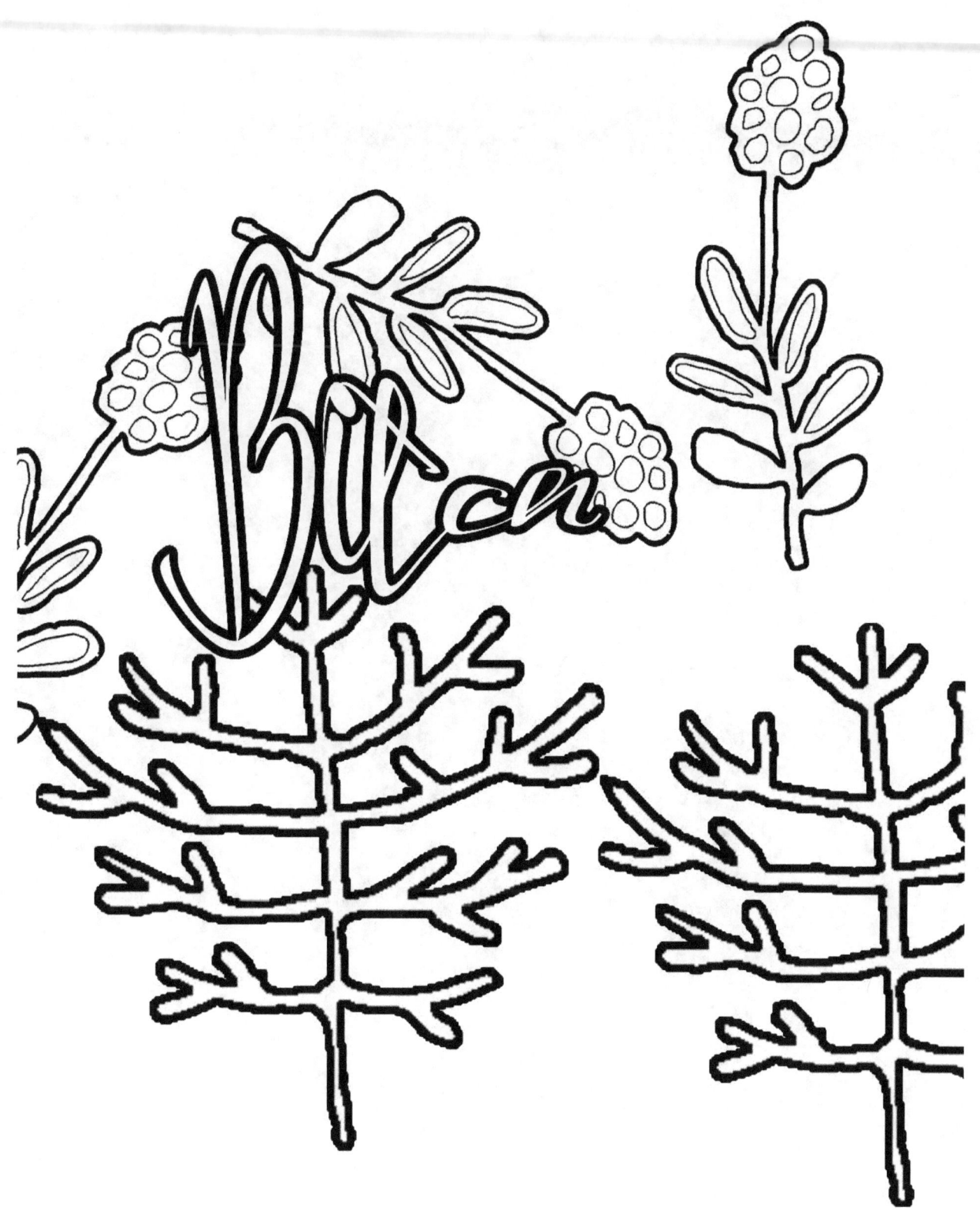

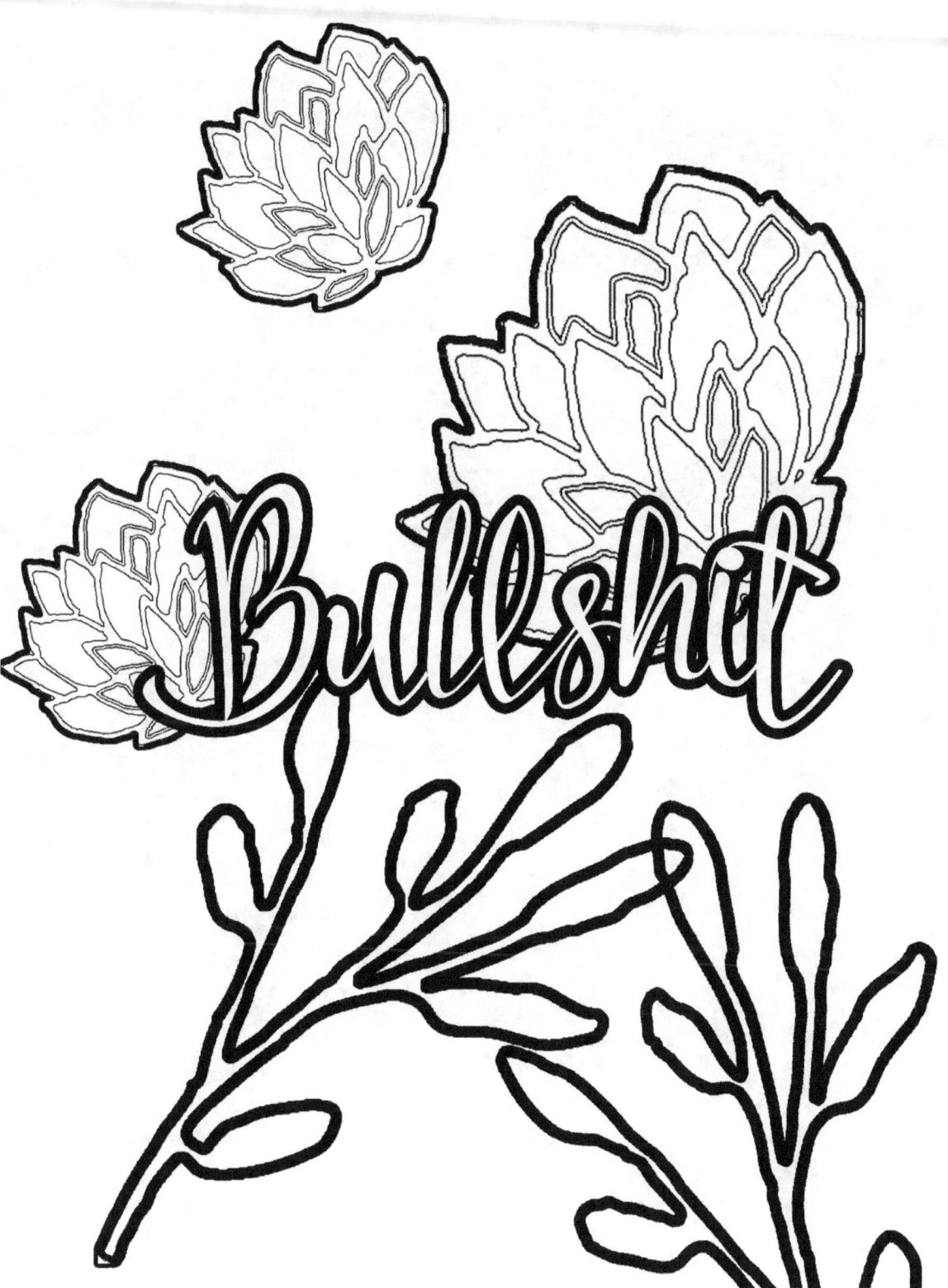

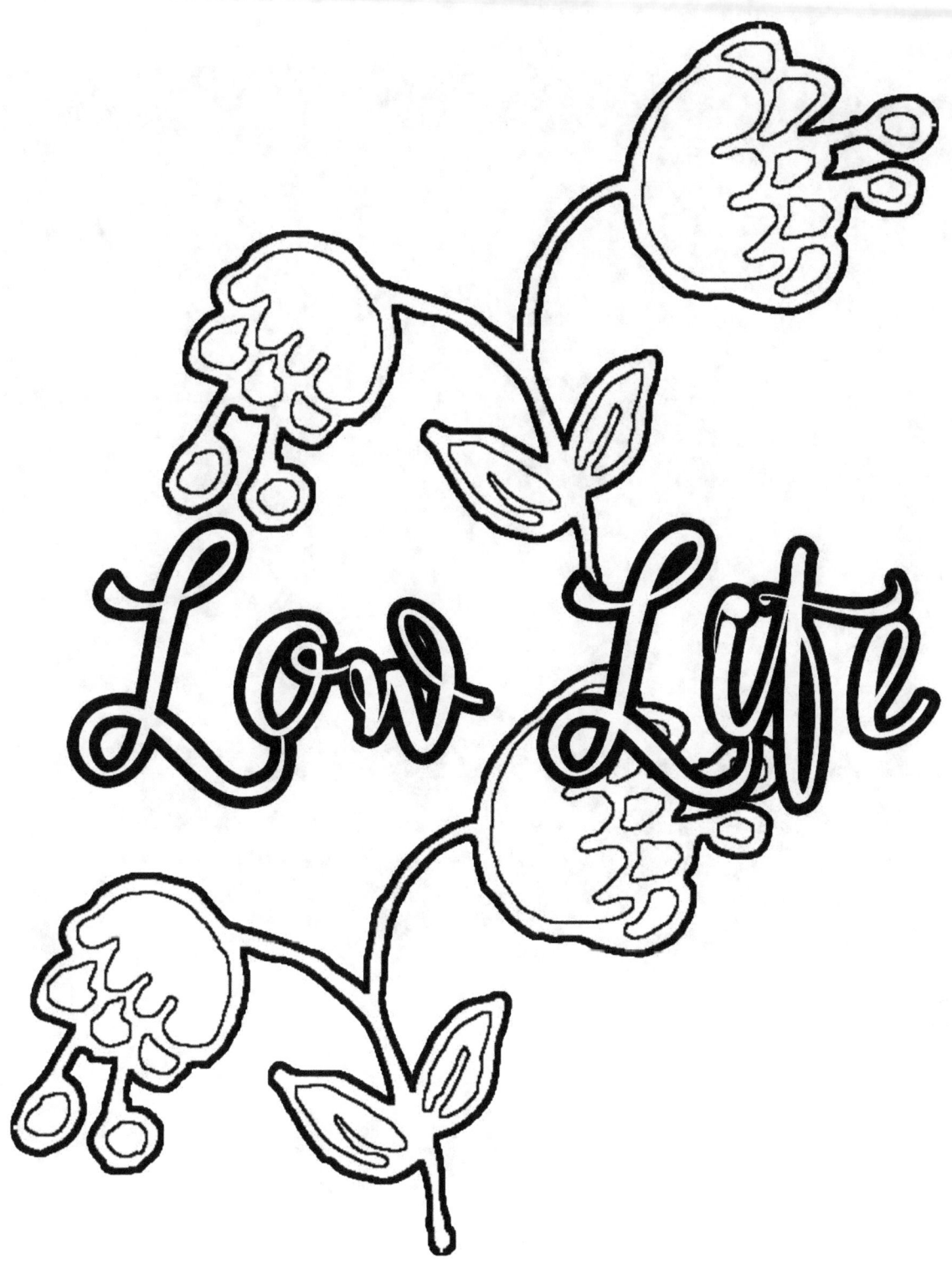

Holy Shit

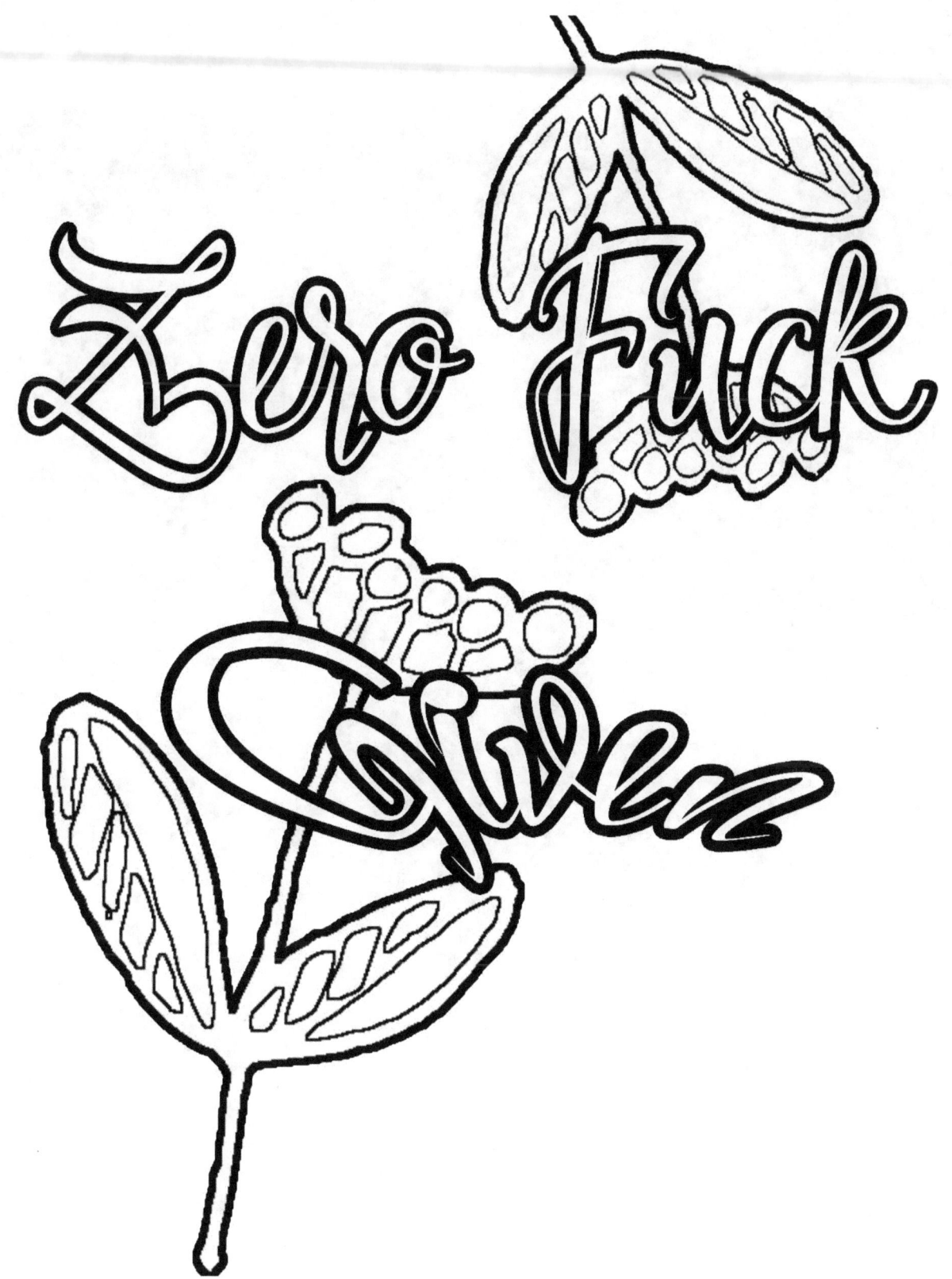

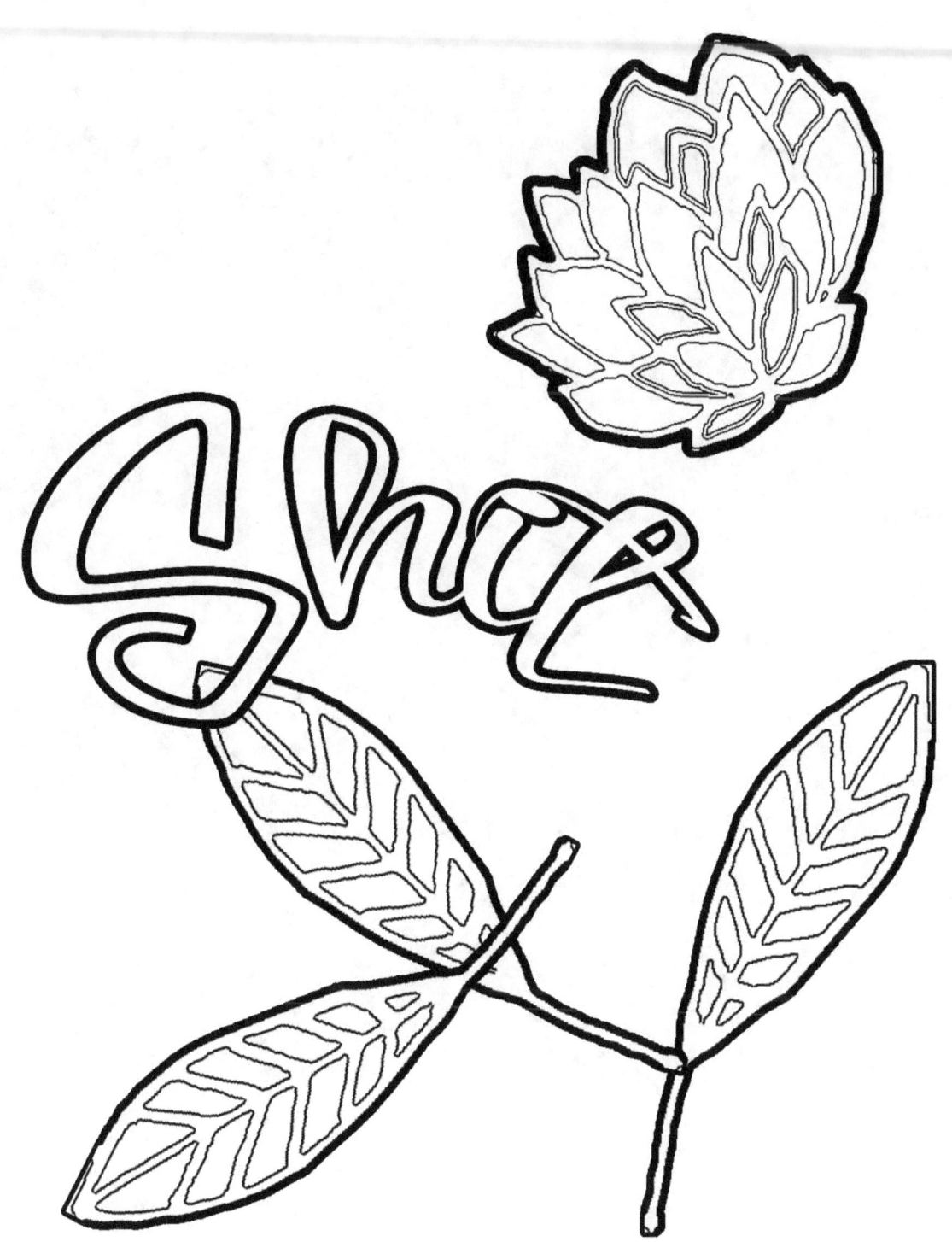

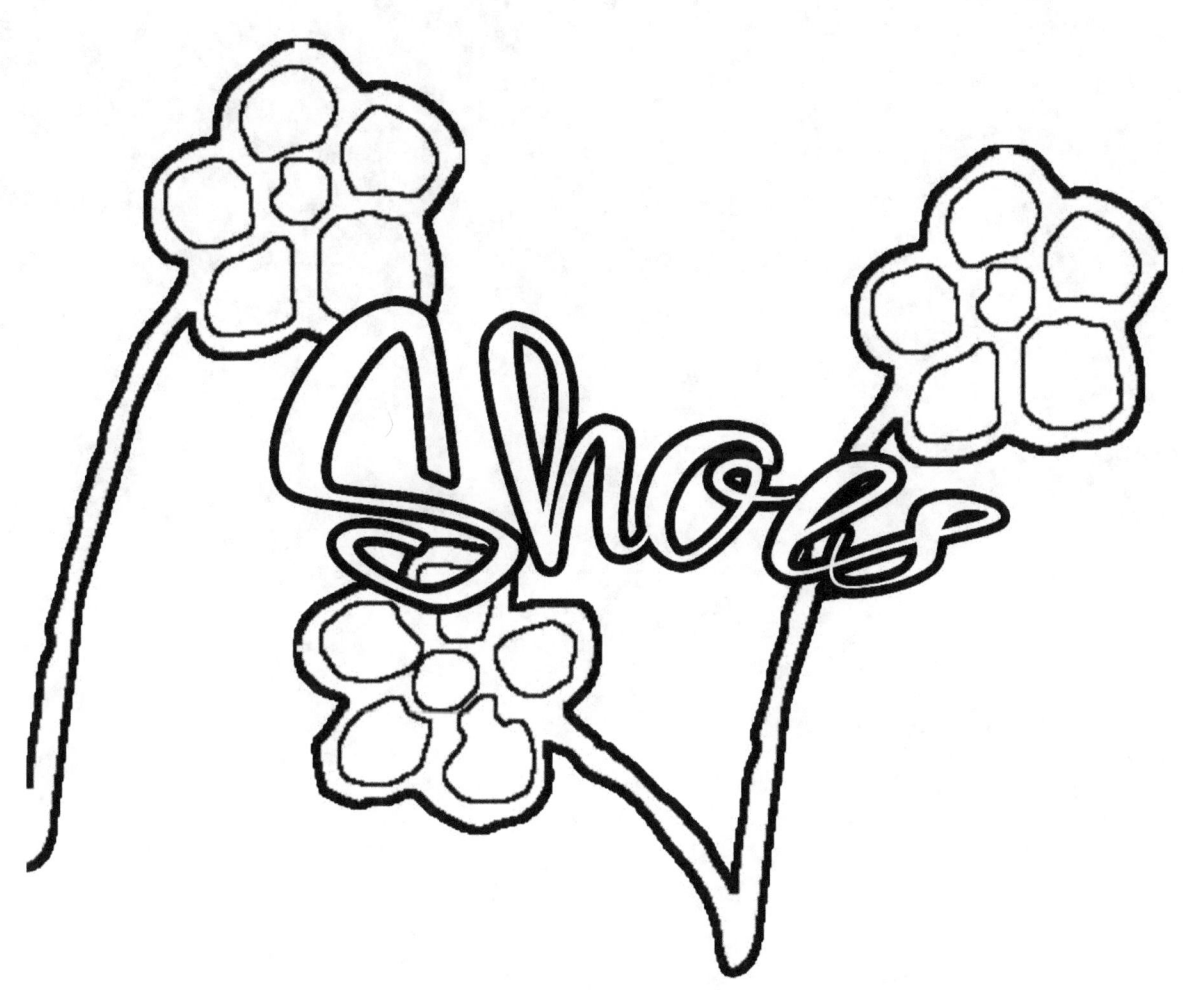

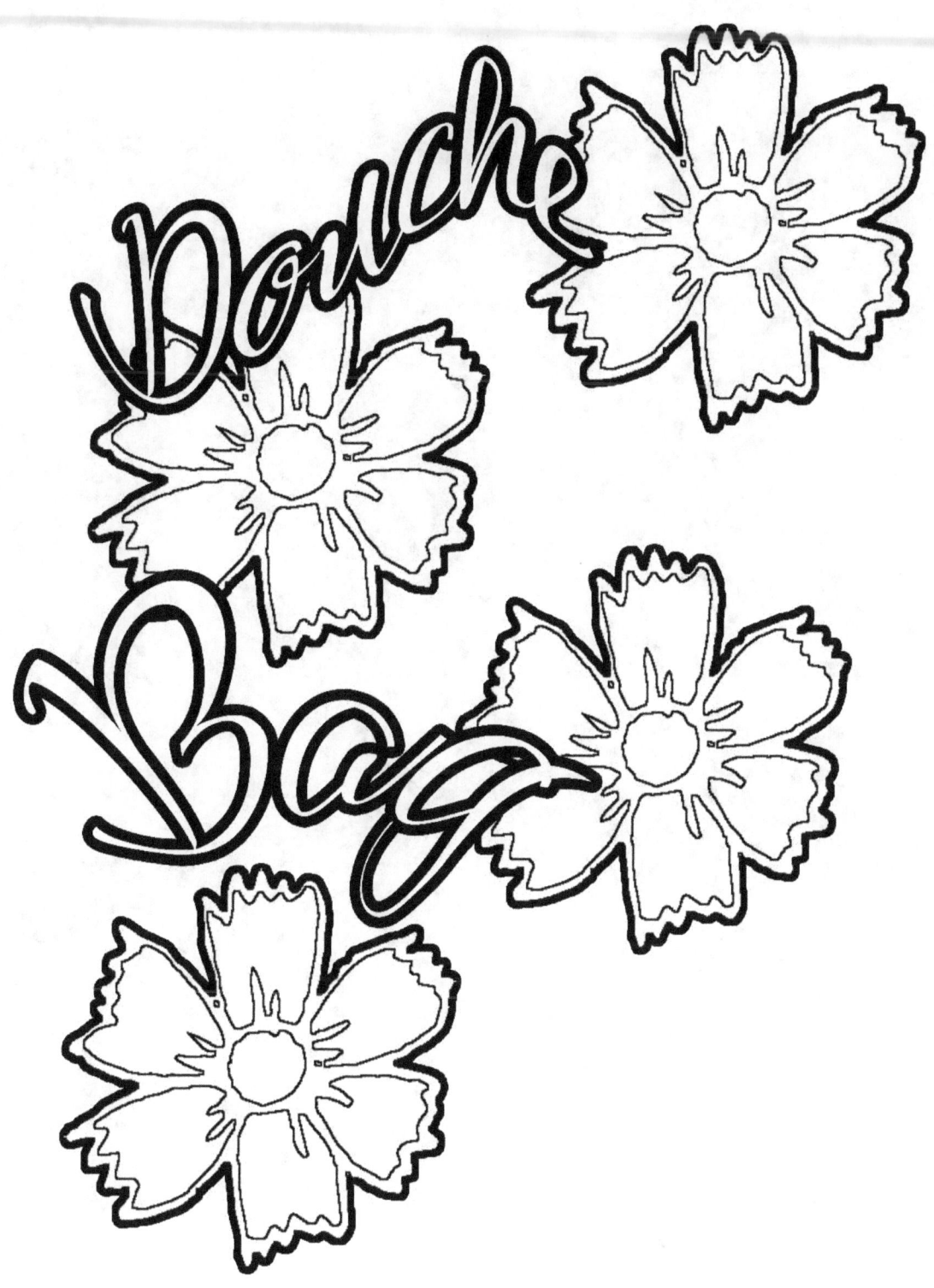

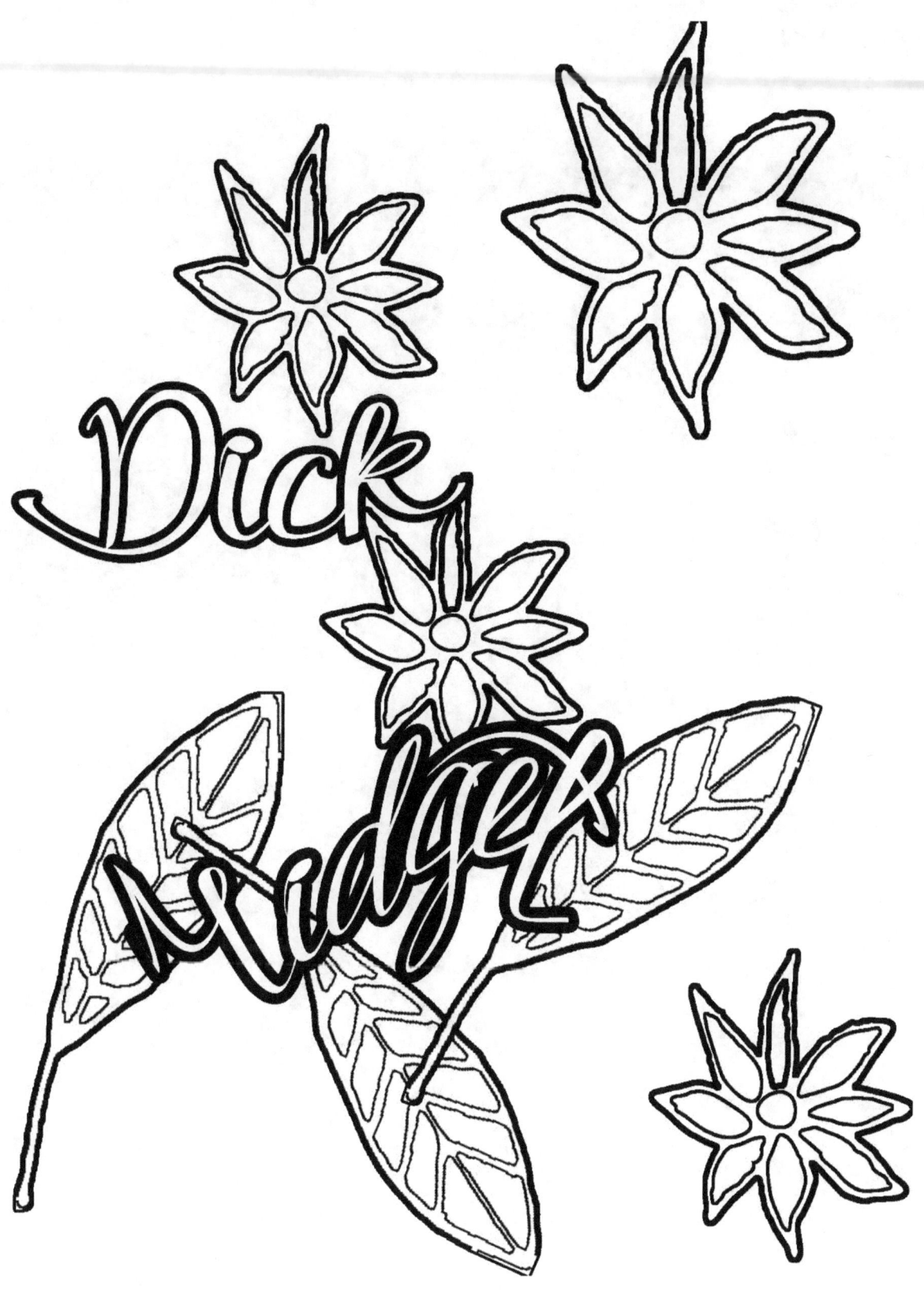

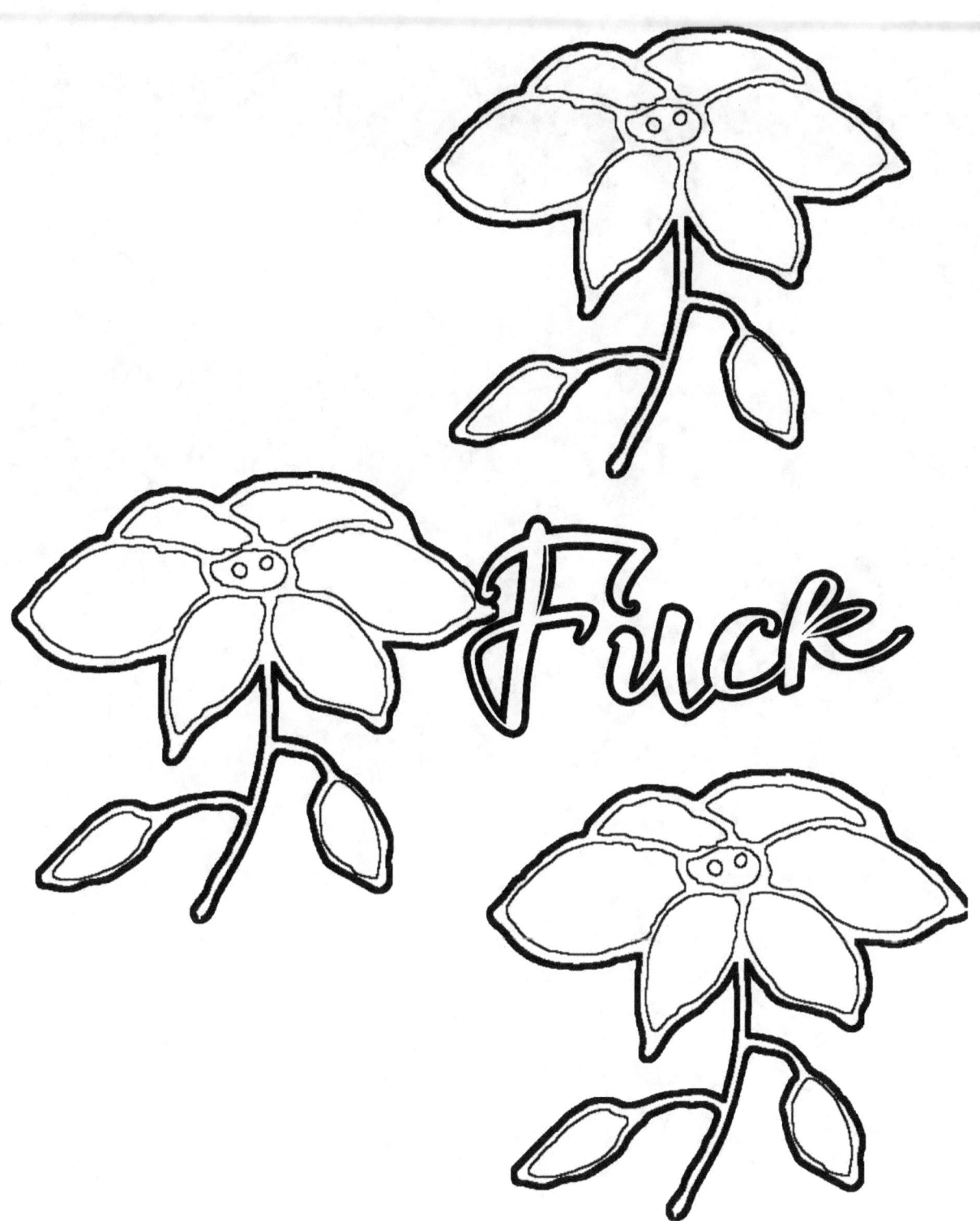

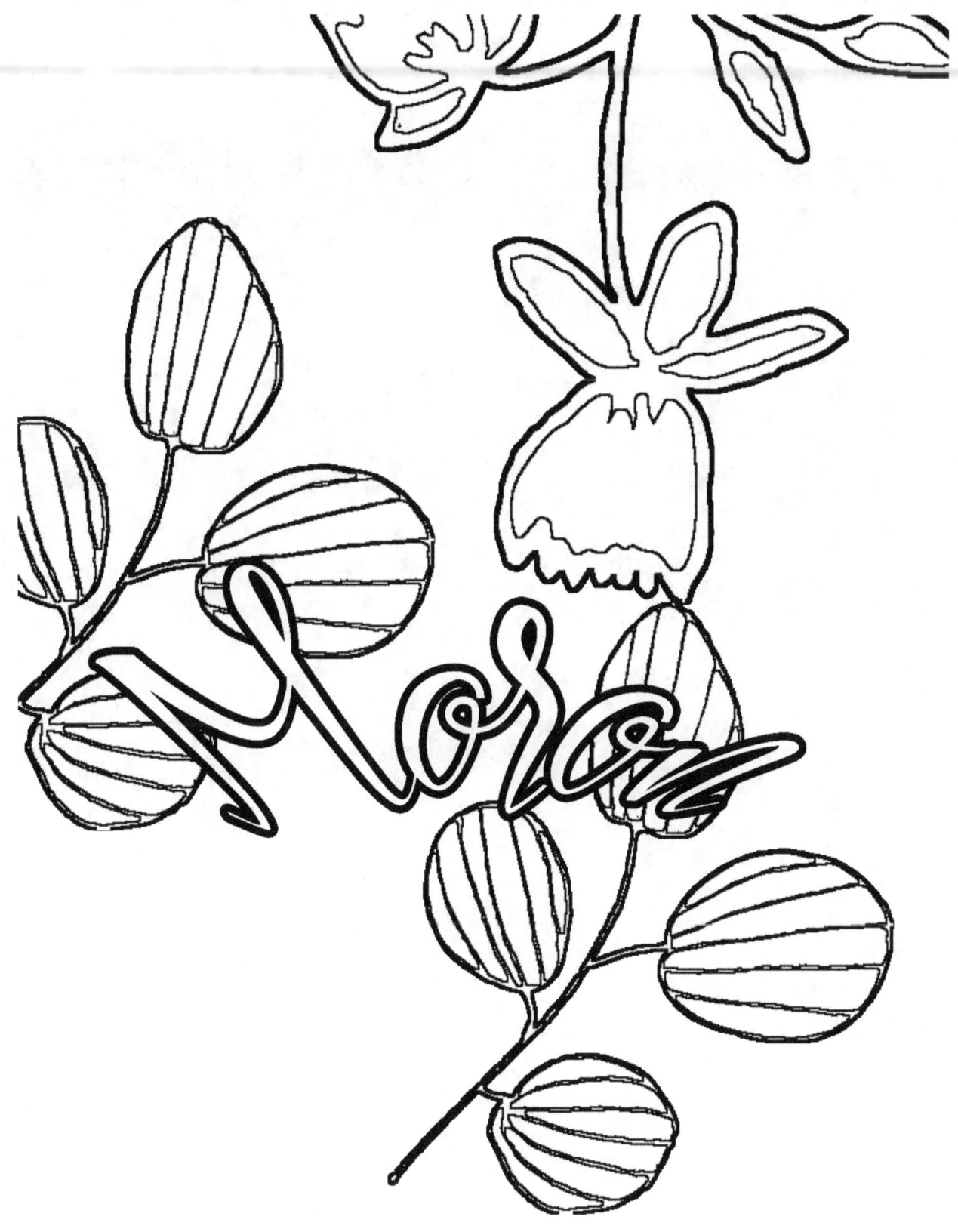

Holly

Fuck

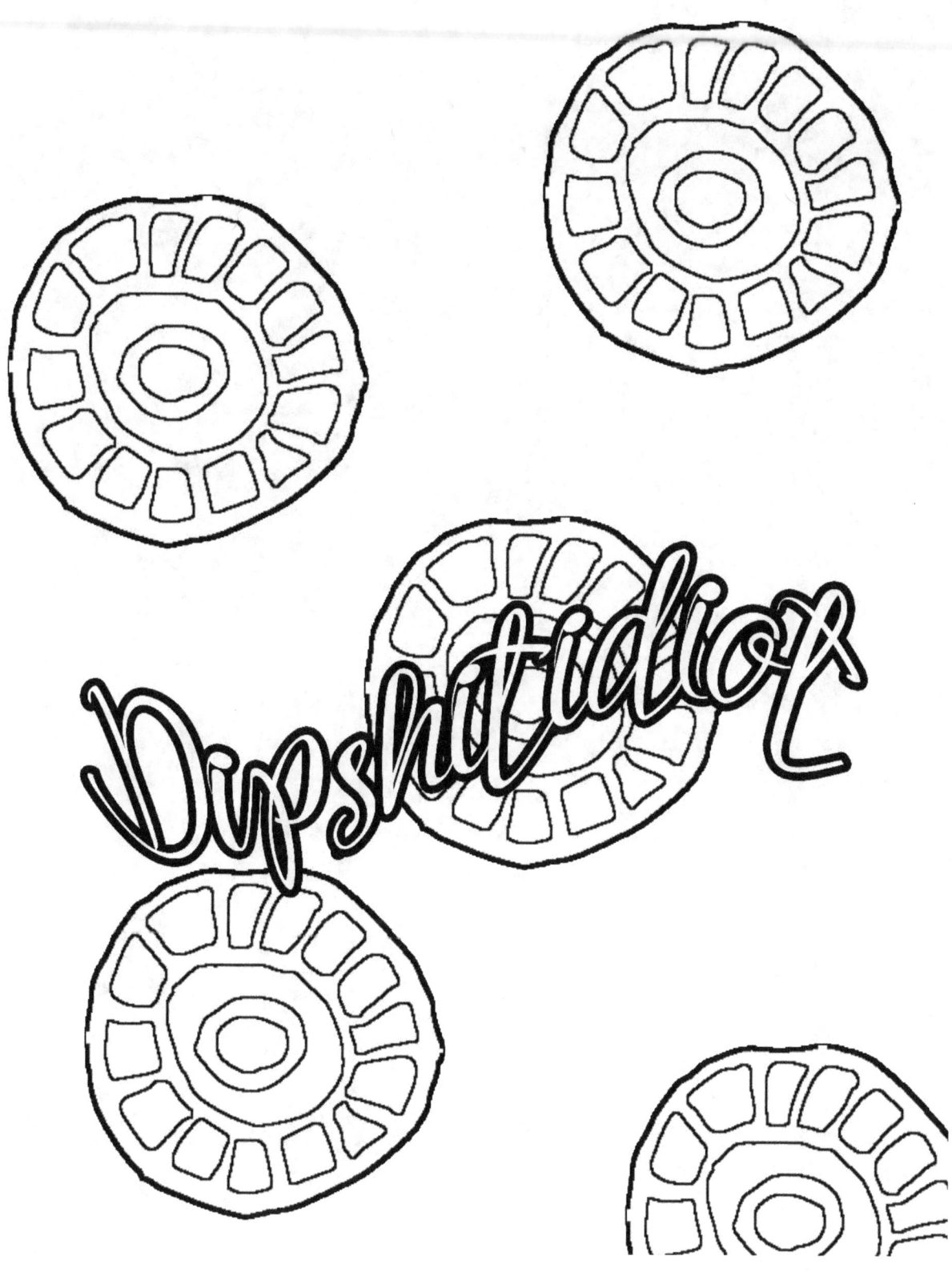

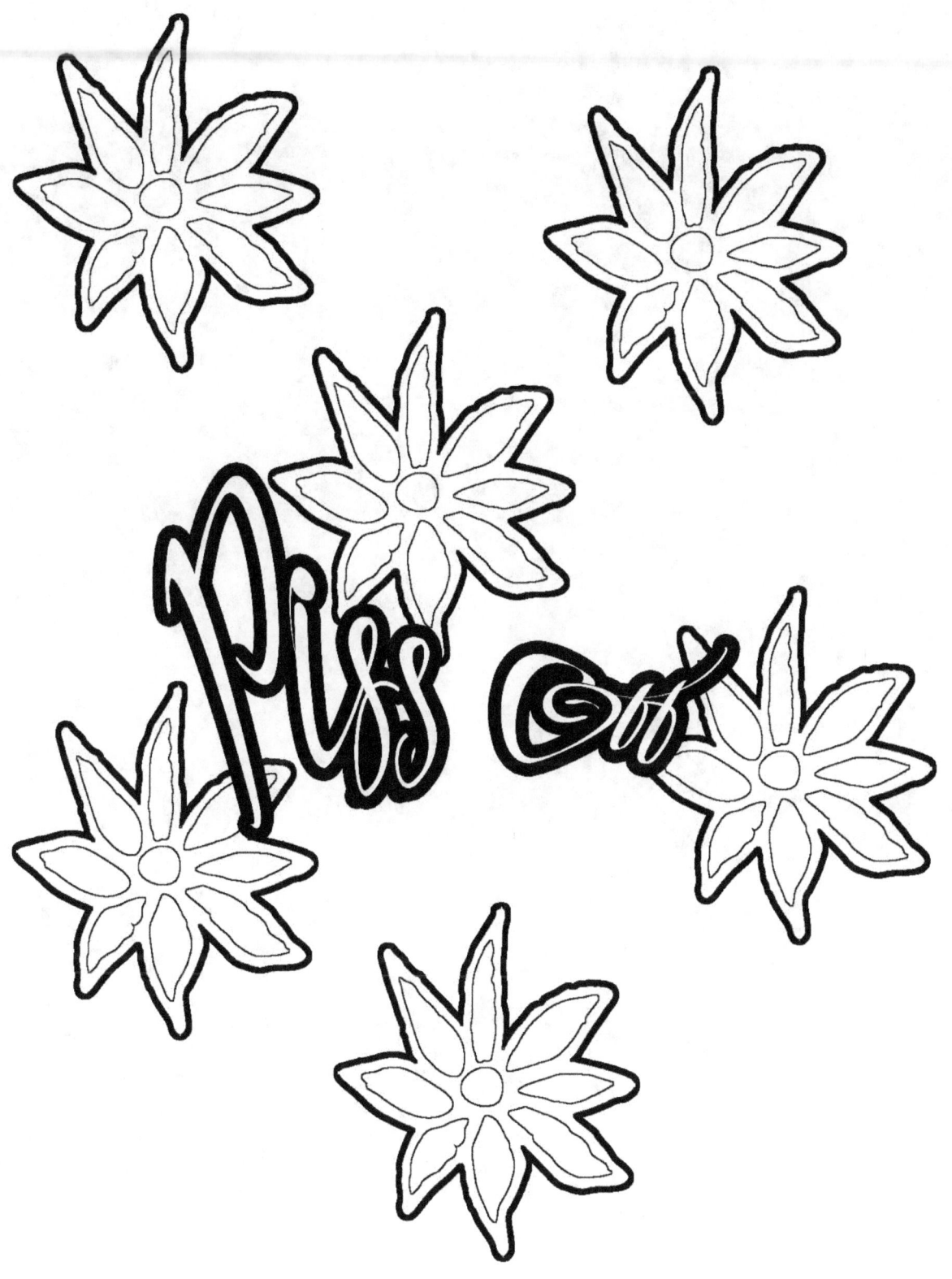

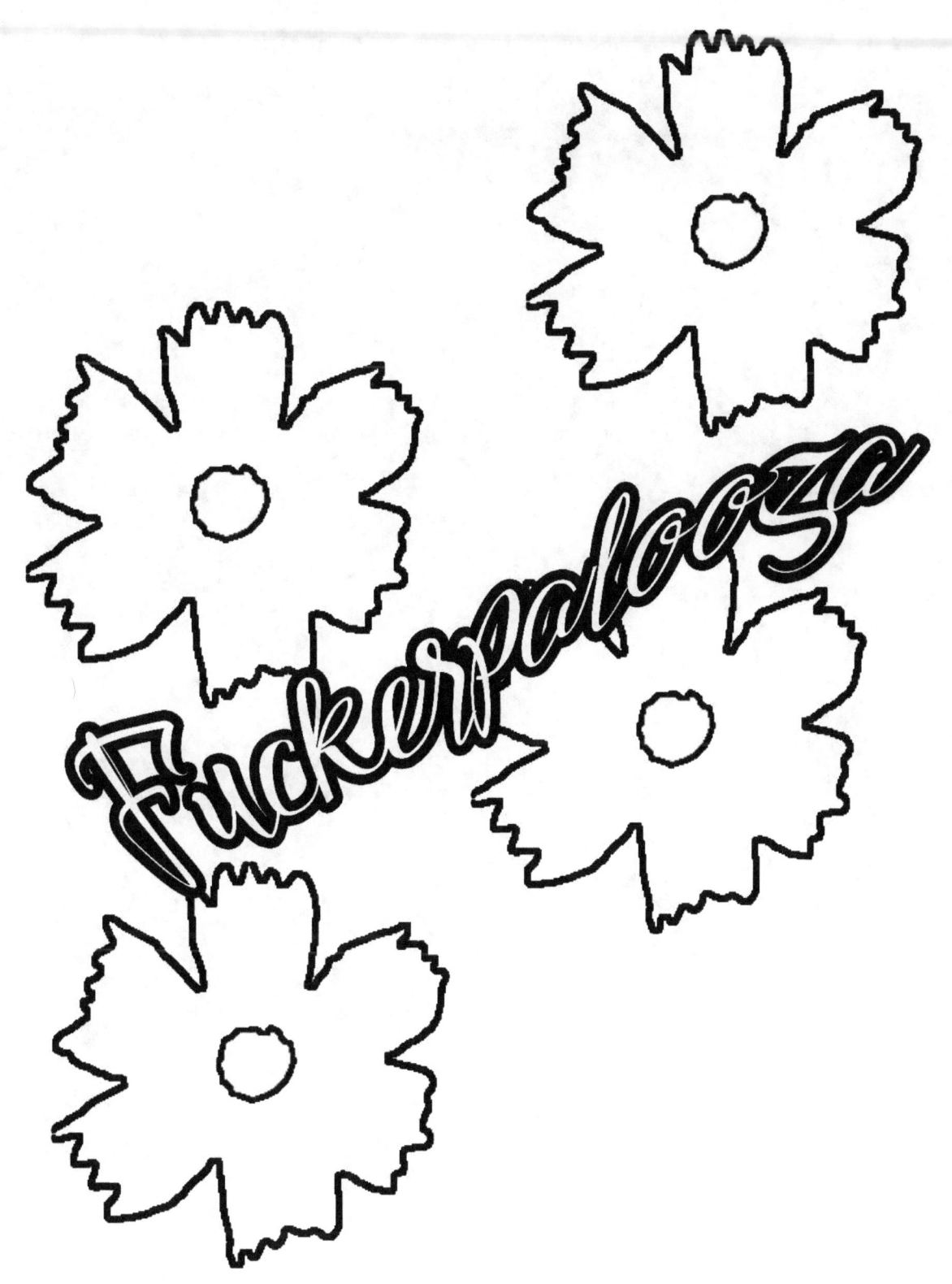

www.ingramcontent.com/pod-product-compliance
Lightning Source LLC
Chambersburg PA
CBHW081123180526
45170CB00008B/2980